MAKE YOUR OWN
CARS, BOATS AND PLANES

Models and text by Brian Edwards
Illustrated by Ron Brown
Photography by Richard Sharpe Studios

INTRODUCTION

Everyone feels good about creating something from nothing and in *Make Your Own* we show you how. Every project has been designed by experts especially for children to make with little or no help from adults. All items are made from materials which are readily found in the home, such as egg boxes, oddments of paper, grocery boxes and cereal packets.

It is not necessary to follow exactly the colours used in this book to decorate the models. Each child should be encouraged to use colours to suit individual taste and at the same time, learn from the simple principles involved in the book how to create other exciting projects.

Best results will be achieved by using the materials as listed and it should be stressed that care should be taken when using certain tools necessary for some projects in this book.

Contents

Whirly~ copter

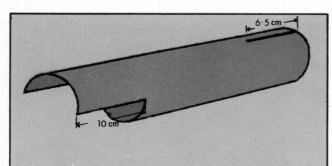

1 Glue down box flaps and cut one end as shown. Use piece cut from one side as a pattern guide for the other.

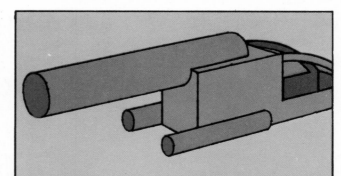

2 Cut pieces of cellophane a bit larger than the holes in box. Glue side pieces inside box. Glue front piece on top. Trim excess.

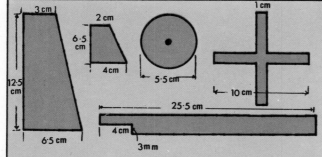

3 Cut parallel slits 10 cm from end of large tube. Cut round half tube and discard section. Cut a 6·5 cm slit in other end.

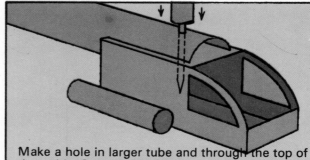

4 Glue thin tube to top of box as shown. Glue 2 small tubes to either side of bottom of box.

5 Cut the above pieces from stiff card. You will need to cut out 4 rotor blades. Make a hole in the circle large enough to take a pencil.

6 Make a hole in larger tube and through the top of the cabin 3 cm from the front. Slide the pencil through. Cut 2·5 cm from a small tube and shape end to fit on larger tube. Glue to tube.

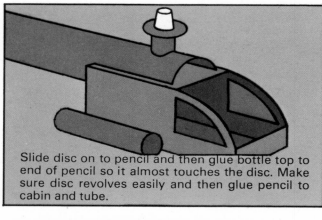

Slide disc on to pencil and then glue bottle top to end of pencil so it almost touches the disc. Make sure disc revolves easily and then glue pencil to cabin and tube.

7

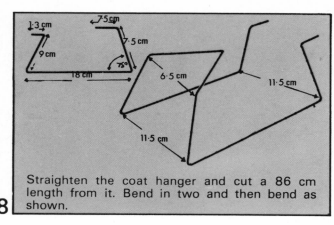

Straighten the coat hanger and cut a 86 cm length from it. Bend in two and then bend as shown.

8

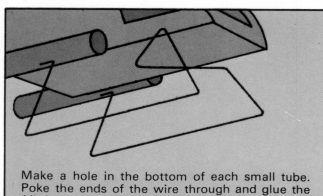

Make a hole in the bottom of each small tube. Poke the ends of the wire through and glue the 'V' shape under the cabin.

9

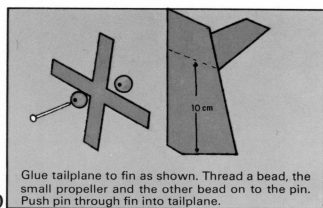

Glue tailplane to fin as shown. Thread a bead, the small propeller and the other bead on to the pin. Push pin through fin into tailplane.

10

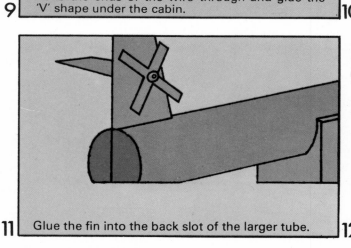

Glue the fin into the back slot of the larger tube.

11

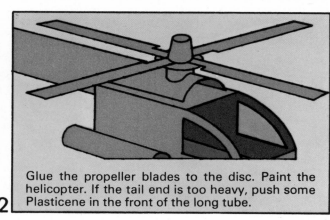

Glue the propeller blades to the disc. Paint the helicopter. If the tail end is too heavy, push some Plasticene in the front of the long tube.

12

Formula Racing Car

YOU WILL NEED:
cardboard box: approx. 30·5 x 7·5 x 3·5 cm
thick card: approx. 15 x 15 cm
4 metal jar lids
2 pieces of wood: approx. 14 x 2 x 2 cm
3 nails 2·5 cm long
hammer · pencil stub · ball pen case
2 rubber bands 5 cm long · countersink bit
2 dowels or pencils 12·5 cm long
glue · scissors · craft knife · paints
matchstick · sticky tape · paper cup
4 wide rubber bands · thin wire:
    approx. 15 cm long

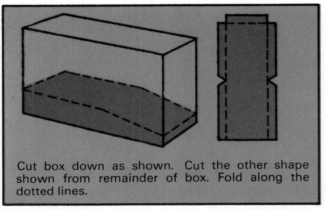

1 Cut box down as shown. Cut the other shape shown from remainder of box. Fold along the dotted lines.

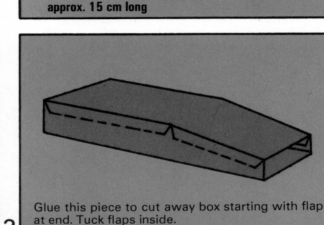

2 Glue this piece to cut away box starting with flap at end. Tuck flaps inside.

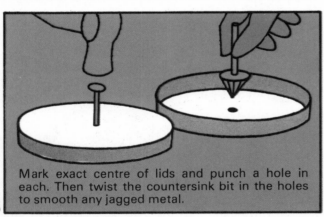

3 Mark exact centre of lids and punch a hole in each. Then twist the countersink bit in the holes to smooth any jagged metal.

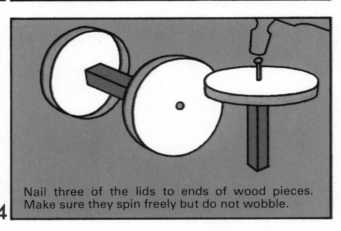

4 Nail three of the lids to ends of wood pieces. Make sure they spin freely but do not wobble.

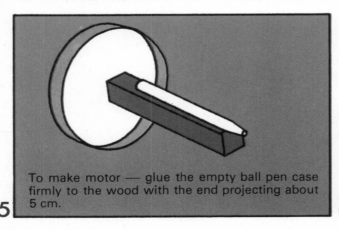

5 To make motor — glue the empty ball pen case firmly to the wood with the end projecting about 5 cm.

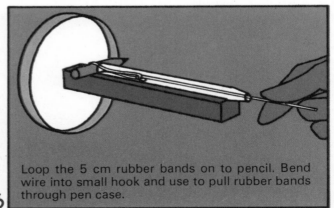

6 Loop the 5 cm rubber bands on to pencil. Bend wire into small hook and use to pull rubber bands through pen case.

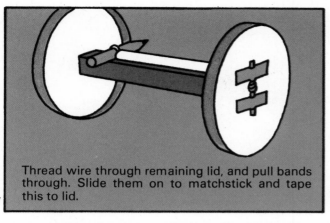

7 Thread wire through remaining lid, and pull bands through. Slide them on to matchstick and tape this to lid.

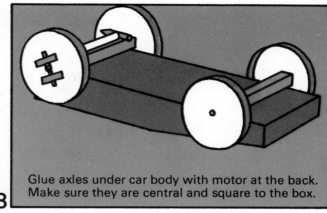

8 Glue axles under car body with motor at the back. Make sure they are central and square to the box.

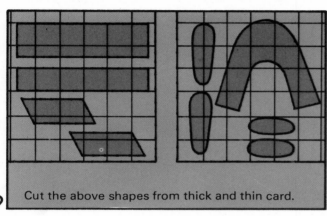

9 Cut the above shapes from thick and thin card.

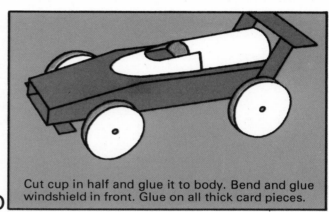

10 Cut cup in half and glue it to body. Bend and glue windshield in front. Glue on all thick card pieces.

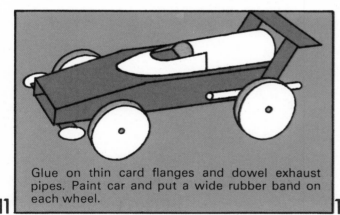

11 Glue on thin card flanges and dowel exhaust pipes. Paint car and put a wide rubber band on each wheel.

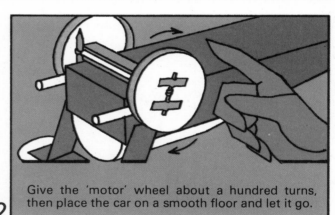

12 Give the 'motor' wheel about a hundred turns, then place the car on a smooth floor and let it go.

Pacific Patrol Ship...

YOU WILL NEED:
shoe box · craft knife · steel rule
thin card: approx. 55 x 27·5 cm · scissors
cardboard box: approx. 9 x 4 x 15 cm
cardboard box: approx. 5 x 2·5 x 12·5 cm
    (both boxes must have opening flaps at
    one end)
cardboard box: approx. 12·5 x 2·5 x 2·5 cm
cardboard tube · pencil, pen or dowel:
    approx. 15 cm
3 spent matchsticks · glue

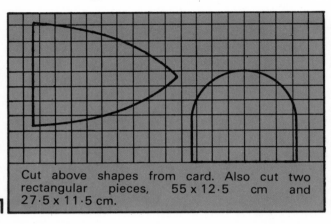

1 Cut above shapes from card. Also cut two rectangular pieces, 55 x 12·5 cm and 27·5 x 11·5 cm.

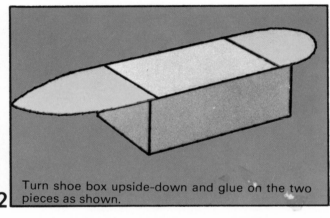

2 Turn shoe box upside-down and glue on the two pieces as shown.

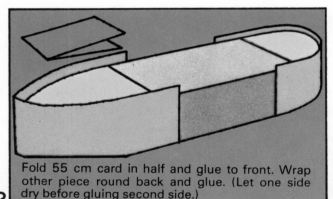

3 Fold 55 cm card in half and glue to front. Wrap other piece round back and glue. (Let one side dry before gluing second side.)

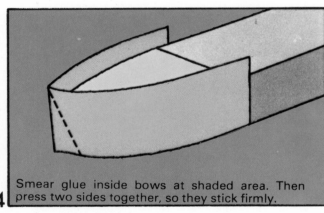

4 Smear glue inside bows at shaded area. Then press two sides together, so they stick firmly.

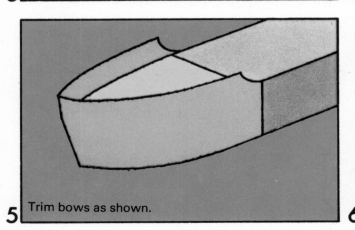

5 Trim bows as shown.

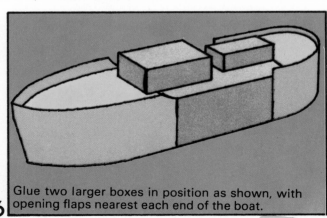

6 Glue two larger boxes in position as shown, with opening flaps nearest each end of the boat.

7 Cut 6·5 cm from tube at an angle and glue, sloping backwards, towards the back of the larger box.

8 Glue remaining box across middle of larger box in front of funnel.

9 Poke pencil through middle of top box. Lean it slightly backwards and glue firmly in position.

10 Glue matches across the top of 'mast'. Now turn over the page for instructions to make the helicopter, lifeboats and guns.

...with Boat, Helicopter and Guns

YOU WILL NEED:
4 small boxes with flaps: approx. 5 x 4 x 1·5 cm
3 drinking straws
4 brass paper clips
glue · scissors · pin · paints
2 pieces of Balsa wood 2·5 x 2·5 x 9 cm
4 wire paper clips · craft knife · pincers
sandpaper · hacksaw blade · table tennis ball
15 amp fuse wire (or similar) · thin card
small cap from toothpaste tube

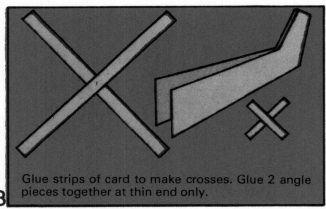

1 Cut above shapes from thin card.

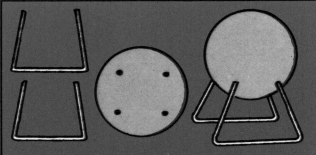

2 Bend two pieces of wire as shown above. Make 4 holes in ball with a pin. Insert wire shapes and glue firmly in place.

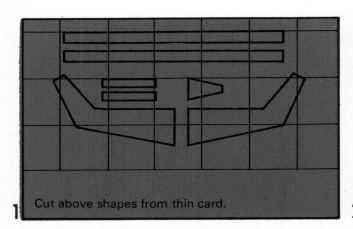

3 Glue strips of card to make crosses. Glue 2 angle pieces together at thin end only.

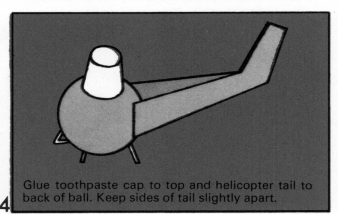

4 Glue toothpaste cap to top and helicopter tail to back of ball. Keep sides of tail slightly apart.

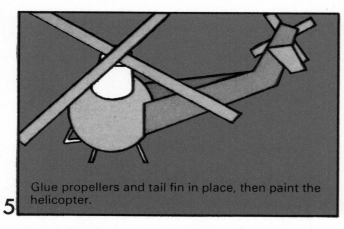

5 Glue propellers and tail fin in place, then paint the helicopter.

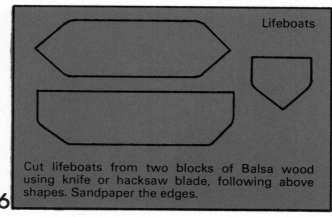

Lifeboats

6 Cut lifeboats from two blocks of Balsa wood using knife or hacksaw blade, following above shapes. Sandpaper the edges.

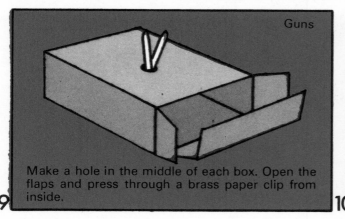

7 Pinch off the small inner hooks from paper clips. Press 2 of the large outer hooks into each lifeboat and glue.

8 Glue lifeboats, by paper clips, to the ship.

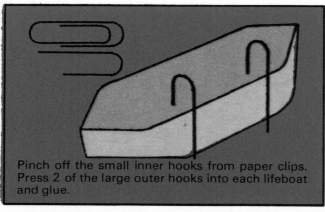

Guns

9 Make a hole in the middle of each box. Open the flaps and press through a brass paper clip from inside.

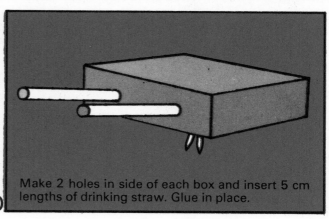

10 Make 2 holes in side of each box and insert 5 cm lengths of drinking straw. Glue in place.

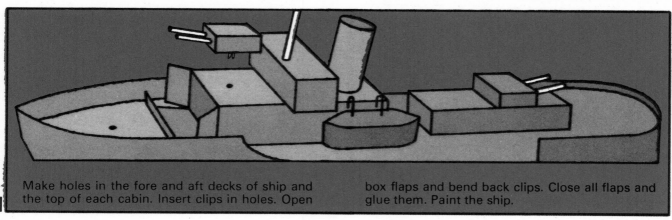

11 Make holes in the fore and aft decks of ship and the top of each cabin. Insert clips in holes. Open box flaps and bend back clips. Close all flaps and glue them. Paint the ship.

Vintage Cars

YOU WILL NEED:
2 cardboard boxes: approx. 3 x 3 x 2·5 cm
1 cardboard box: approx. 5 x 3 x 3·5 cm
1 cardboard box: approx. 4 x 3 x 6 cm
1 cardboard box: approx. 5 x 3 x 3 cm
stiff card · drinking straw
4 cocktail sticks · kitchen foil
scissors · glue

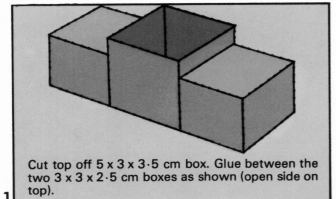

1 Cut top off 5 x 3 x 3·5 cm box. Glue between the two 3 x 3 x 2·5 cm boxes as shown (open side on top).

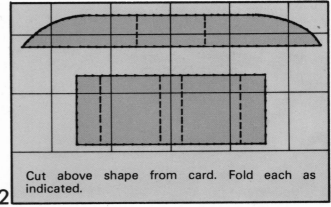

2 Cut above shape from card. Fold each as indicated.

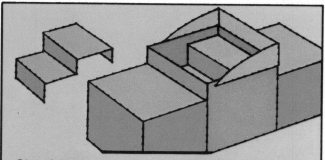

Glue folded rectangle into middle box to make seat. Glue strip to outside back of middle box to make a 'folded down hood'.

3

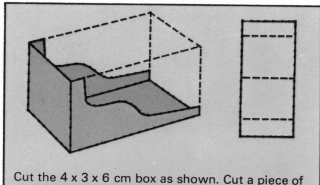

Cut the 4 x 3 x 6 cm box as shown. Cut a piece of card 6 x 3 cm and bend as indicated.

4

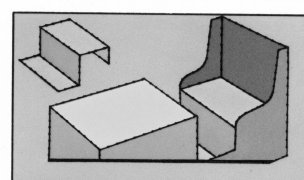

Glue cut box to remaining box as shown. Glue in piece of folded card to make seat.

5

Cut out 'windscreens' from card and glue to cars.

6

Cut 8 circles 2·5 cm in diameter from card. Paint circles and cars.

7

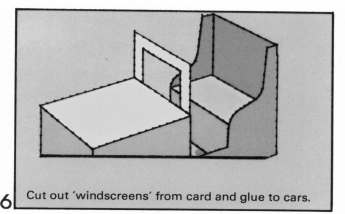

Make holes with cocktail sticks at front and back at bottom of boxes. Push sticks through boxes. Slide on circles. Secure ends with foil balls.

8

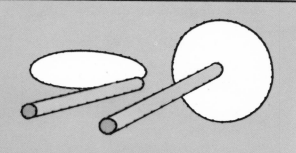

Cut 2 circles 1·5 cm in diameter. Cut 5 cm and 2 cm lengths from straw. Cut ends as shown. Glue circles to top end to make steering wheel.

9

Glue steering column to car. Glue 4 card strips, 5 cm long, to smaller car for mudguards.

10

17

Faster than Sound Jetplane

YOU WILL NEED:
thin cardboard tube: approx. 23 x 4 cm
cardboard tube: approx. 13 x 2 cm
thick card: approx. 30 x 25 cm
Plasticene · nail · gummed paper tape
3 cocktail sticks · kitchen knife
Emulsion paint · craft knife · steel rule
small clear plastic flat-sided bottle
strong glue · scissors · 2·5 cm brush
paints · fine sandpaper

1 Cut the above shapes from the card.

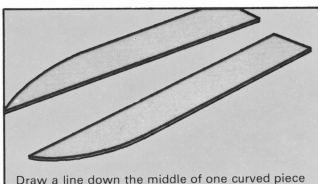

2 Draw a line down the middle of one curved piece and cut it in half.

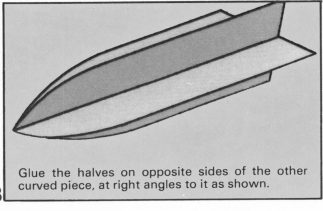

3 Glue the halves on opposite sides of the other curved piece, at right angles to it as shown.

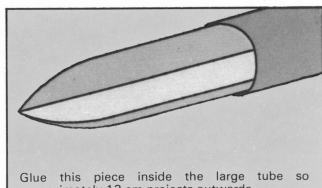

4 Glue this piece inside the large tube so approximately 13 cm projects outwards.

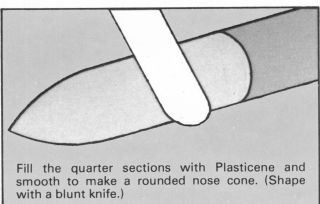

5 Fill the quarter sections with Plasticene and smooth to make a rounded nose cone. (Shape with a blunt knife.)

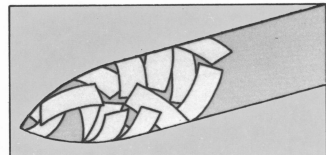

6 Stick strips of gummed tape over Plasticene. When dry, repeat twice more keeping tape as flat as possible.

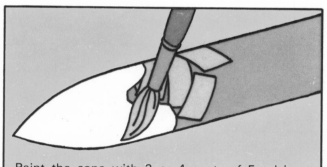

7 Paint the cone with 3 or 4 coats of Emulsion, sanding down with fine sandpaper between coats.

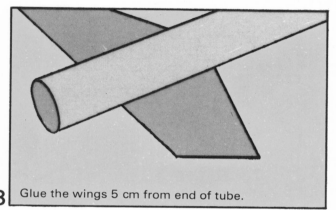

8 Glue the wings 5 cm from end of tube.

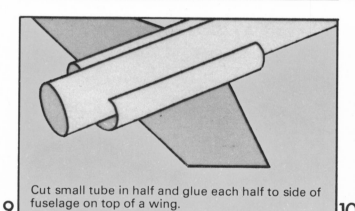

9 Cut small tube in half and glue each half to side of fuselage on top of a wing.

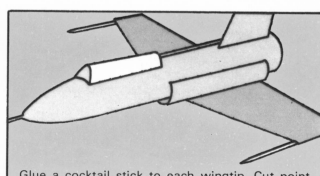

10 Glue the 2 tailpieces in place.

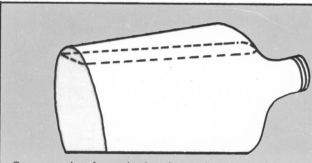

11 Cut a portion from the bottle as shown and glue it to fuselage. Shape ends of bottle to fit curve properly.

12 Glue a cocktail stick to each wingtip. Cut point from remaining stick, and glue into nose tip. Paint plane.

Red Super~ Streak

YOU WILL NEED:
thick card: approx. 30 x 38 cm
thin card: approx. 15 x 45 cm
2 cardboard boxes: approx. 10 x 214 x 715 cm
dowel or straight bamboo cane 1 x 2 cm
4 jar lids 5·5 cm diameter · strong glue
oil paints · brushes · craft knife
steel rule · sandpaper · protractor
saw · Sellotape

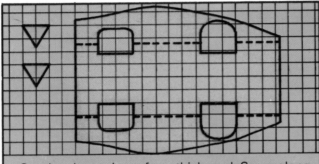

1 Cut the above shape from thick card. Score along fold lines with knife and fold. Cut 2 equilateral triangles, with 5 cm sides.

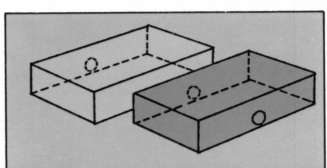

2 Cut round holes 1 cm diameter in long sides of boxes at bottom. Make sure they align with one another.

3 Cut 2 pieces of dowel 11 cm long, making sure cuts are square. Push through box holes and wind tape on to ends to hold in place.

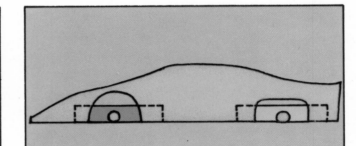

4 Glue boxes on to chassis. Make sure dowels are centred in wheel holes when car is viewed from the side.

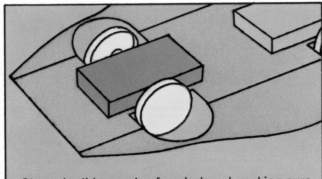

5 Glue a jar lid to ends of each dowel, making sure they are all centred properly.

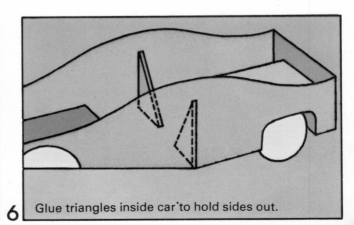

6 Glue triangles inside car to hold sides out.

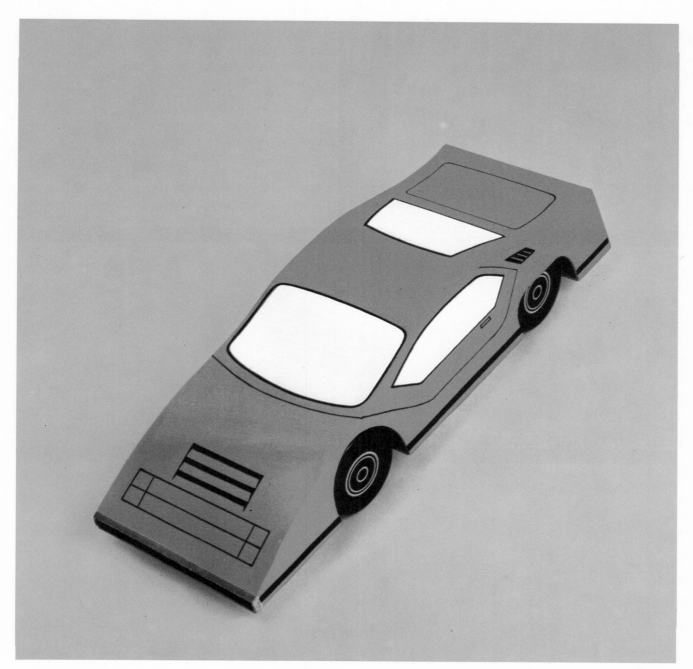

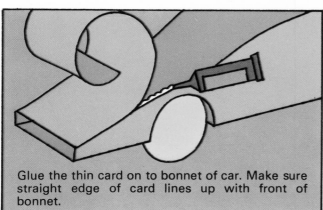

7 Glue the thin card on to bonnet of car. Make sure straight edge of card lines up with front of bonnet.

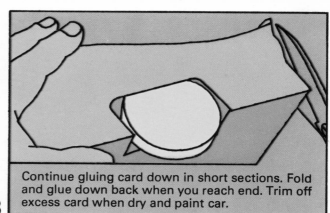

8 Continue gluing card down in short sections. Fold and glue down back when you reach end. Trim off excess card when dry and paint car.

Tip-up Truck

YOU WILL NEED:
cardboard box: approx. 9 x 11 x 5 cm
cardboard box: approx. 18 x 3 x 4 cm
cardboard box: approx. 11 x 3 x 4 cm
plastic food dish: approx. 12·5 x 8 x 18 cm
4 jar lids: approx. 8 cm diameter · strong thread
2 round pencils or dowels 10 cm long
thick wire: approx. 15 cm long · Sellotape
pliers · craft knife · scissors
thick card: approx. 20 x 4 cm · drinking straw
4 cotton reels or plastic bottle caps
scissors · strong glue · fine saw · pencil and ruler

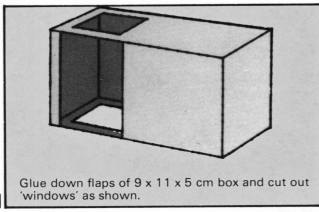

1 Glue down flaps of 9 x 11 x 5 cm box and cut out 'windows' as shown.

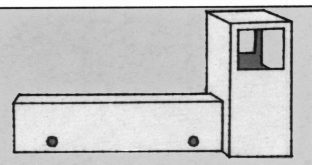

2 Cut 2 holes on each side of 18 x 3 x 4 cm box just large enough to take pencils. Glue bottom of box to middle of cab.

3 Poke pencils or dowels through holes. Glue a cotton reel on each end near box. If pencils are too thin, bind with Sellotape.

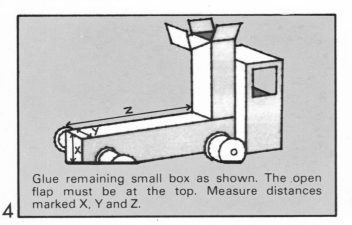

4 Glue remaining small box as shown. The open flap must be at the top. Measure distances marked X, Y and Z.

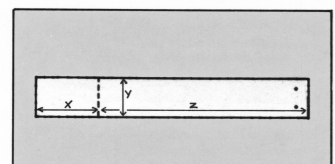

5 Cut a piece of thick card to same dimensions as X, Y and Z. Score and fold along dotted line. Make 2 small holes at other end.

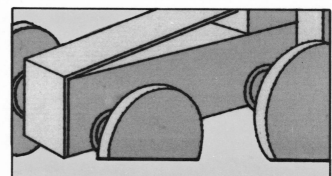

6 Glue card to *end* of box (not to top). Glue a jar lid on each cotton reel, making sure they are central.

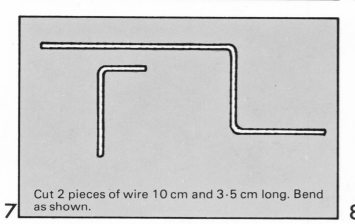

7 Cut 2 pieces of wire 10 cm and 3·5 cm long. Bend as shown.

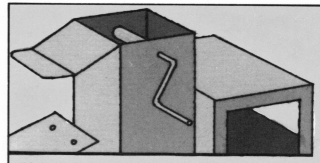

8 Make holes each side of upright box and insert wire handle. Thicken by binding with Sellotape. Cut off side flaps of box.

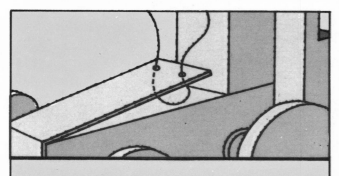

9 Cut a hole in box lid. Push thread down through one hole in thick card and up through the other.

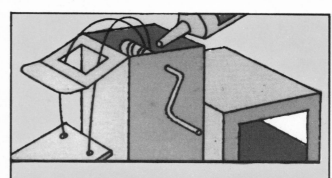

10 Poke thread through box flap and glue ends to handle. Glue down the flap.

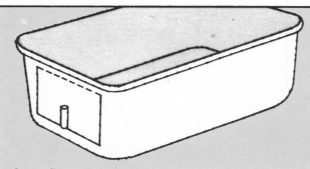

11 Cut a flap at one end of plastic dish. Bend along dotted line. (If it won't bend, cut off and tape on.) Glue 1 cm of drinking straw as shown.

12 Glue dish on to thick card and paint truck. Slot wire catch into drinking straw. Fill tipper with sand, release catch and wind handle.

Hydroplane

YOU WILL NEED:
flat plastic bottle: approx. 10 cm long
ball pen case · electrician's tape
piece of thin tin 8 cm square
scissors · paper clips
strong waterproof glue
rubber band · thin wire 15 cm long
pliers · short pencil · compass or dividers
long plastic bottle cap · fine saw
set square · hammer and nail · file or
   countersink bit · oil paints

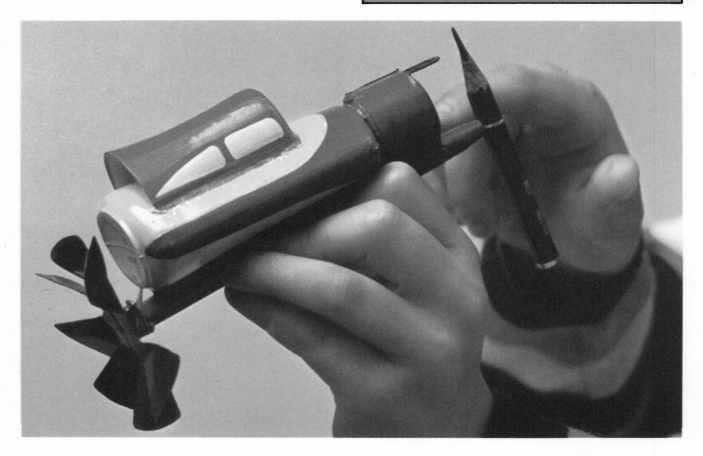

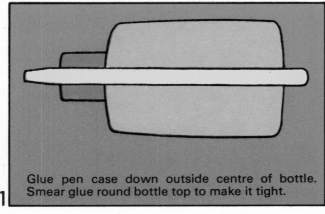

1 Glue pen case down outside centre of bottle. Smear glue round bottle top to make it tight.

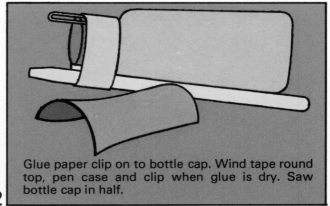

2 Glue paper clip on to bottle cap. Wind tape round top, pen case and clip when glue is dry. Saw bottle cap in half.

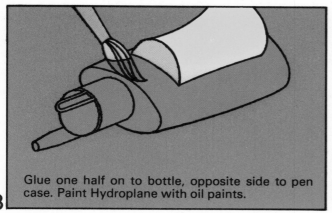

3 Glue one half on to bottle, opposite side to pen case. Paint Hydroplane with oil paints.

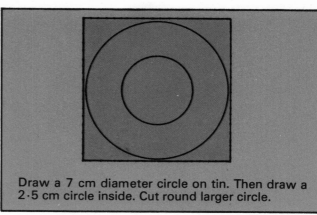

4 Draw a 7 cm diameter circle on tin. Then draw a 2·5 cm circle inside. Cut round larger circle.

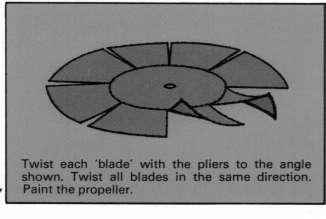

5 Punch a small hole in centre of circle. Smooth edges of hole with the bit or a file.

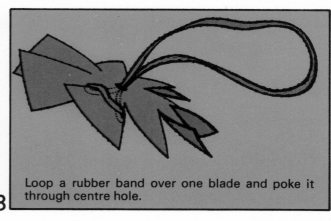

6 Using a set square and nail, draw lines round tin and cut each one as far as the inner circle.

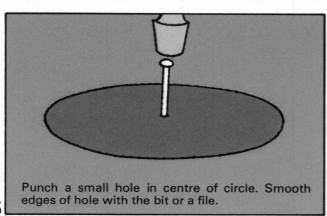

7 Twist each 'blade' with the pliers to the angle shown. Twist all blades in the same direction. Paint the propeller.

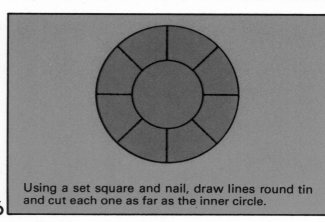

8 Loop a rubber band over one blade and poke it through centre hole.

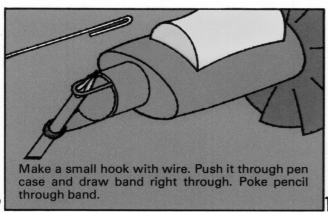

9 Make a small hook with wire. Push it through pen case and draw band right through. Poke pencil through band.

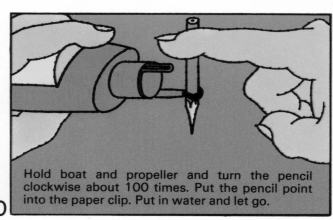

10 Hold boat and propeller and turn the pencil clockwise about 100 times. Put the pencil point into the paper clip. Put in water and let go.

IBP Star~Finder Rocket

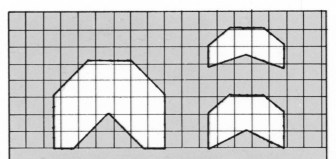

1 Cut two of each of these shapes from the card. Start by drawing rectangles and mark the centre with a pencil line.

2 Take one pair of cards and cut a slit half way down the centre panel on one card and half way up the other card. Repeat on each pair.

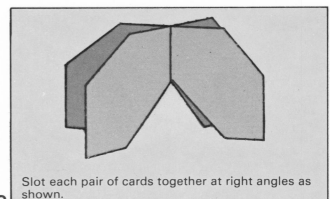

3 Slot each pair of cards together at right angles as shown.

YOU WILL NEED:
2 thin cardboard tubes: approx. 23 x 4 cm
ruler · pencil
silver and black paint
glue · scissors
thin stiff card 30·5 x 30·5 cm
orange and blue paper
paper 15 x 15 cm

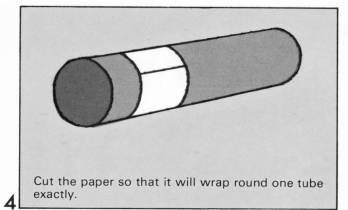

4 Cut the paper so that it will wrap round one tube exactly.

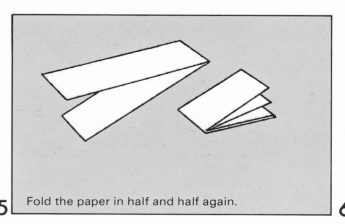

5 Fold the paper in half and half again.

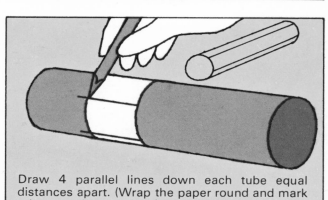

6 Draw 4 parallel lines down each tube equal distances apart. (Wrap the paper round and mark tube at each paper fold.)

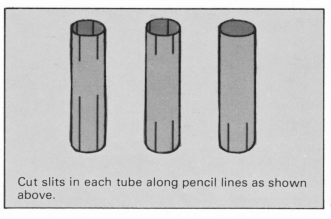

7 Cut slits in each tube along pencil lines as shown above.

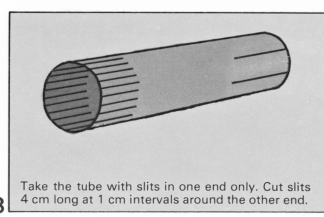

8 Take the tube with slits in one end only. Cut slits 4 cm long at 1 cm intervals around the other end.

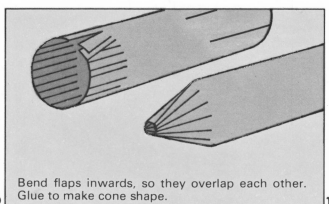

9 Bend flaps inwards, so they overlap each other. Glue to make cone shape.

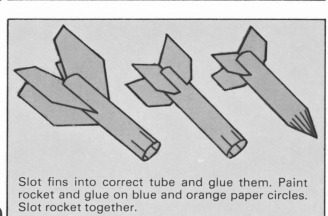

10 Slot fins into correct tube and glue them. Paint rocket and glue on blue and orange paper circles. Slot rocket together.

Mediaeval Privateer

YOU WILL NEED:
wood (preferably Balsa): 11 x 2·5 x 2·5 cm
thick card or Balsa wood: 6 x 6 x 0·25 cm
thick white paper: 18 x 15 cm
thick card: 7·5 x 2·5 cm · postcard
strong box or tin lid: approx. 20 x 15 x 2·5 cm
12 cocktail sticks · black thread · pencil
model aircraft dope · craft knife · ruler
paints and brushes · fine saw · sharp scissors
glue · file · sandpaper · tweezers
small tube · small round nail
household candle

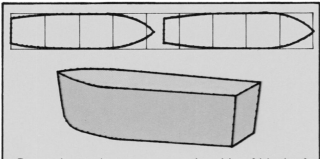

1 Draw above shapes on opposite side of block of wood. (Square end level with end of wood.) Cut and file hull shape. File bottom of bows.

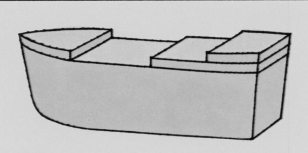

2 Glue pieces of 0·25 Balsa or card on to deck as shown. Edges across deck must be square with hull. Sand pieces flush to hull and paint.

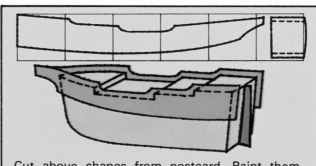

3 Cut above shapes from postcard. Paint them. Glue rudder to ship. Glue on sides so they overlap hull. Glue bows together.

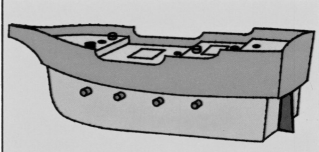

4 Fold and glue rear piece in place. Add guns, hatches and capstans from card and tiny bits of cocktail stick. Make holes in decks for masts.

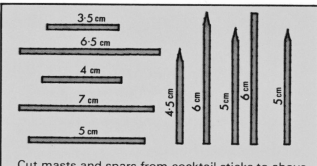

5 Cut masts and spars from cocktail sticks to above measurements. Note some ends are tapered. Glue main mast together. Paint pieces.

3·5 cm
6·5 cm
4 cm
7 cm
5 cm

4·5 cm 6 cm 5 cm 6 cm 5 cm

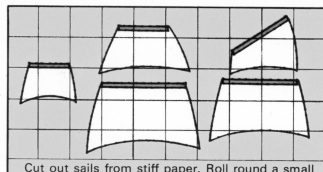

6 Cut out sails from stiff paper. Roll round a small tube so they appear to billow. Glue them to corresponding spars.

7 Glue spars to mast. Glue masts into holes in deck. Set at angles indicated. Check masts are upright and in line.

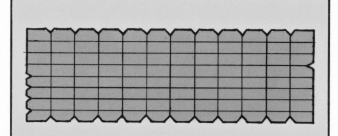

8 Measure and draw lines shown on 7·5 x 2·5 cm card. Cut tiny notches at ends of each line, except bottom upright. Rub card with candle.

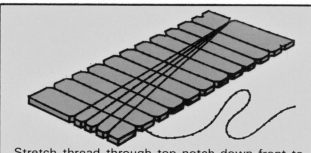

9 Stretch thread through top notch down front to 1st bottom notch, back up, down front to 2nd. Repeat to 3rd and 4th, then along horizontal lines.

10 Cut and paint 6 bits of stick 1 cm long. Dope thread. Glue stick in place on rigging and cut from card. Make 2 more from front of card.

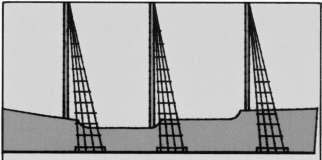

11 Make 3 sets of rigging using reverse of card. Trim ends and glue to masts and sides of hull, so rigging slopes backwards.

12 Squeeze glue to box lid to make waves. Paint blue. Glue on galleon. Add white paint 'foam'. Cut out, paint and glue on pennants.

Look~Out Car

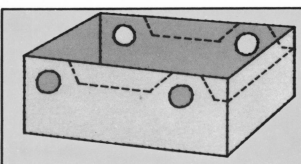

1 Make 2 holes on each side of shoe box, same size as tubes. Ensure each pair line up, then cut down sides of box as shown.

2 Cut 2·5 cm from 17·5 cm tube. The other tubes should be equal to width of shoe box plus depth of two jar lids.

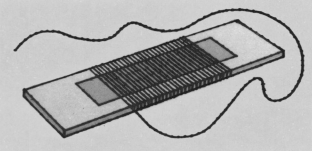

3 Cut a piece of card 5 x 1·25 cm and wind fuse wire round middle. Leave 45 cm of spare wire. Sellotape one side of card.

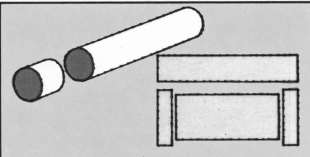

4 Make 1·25 cm slots each side of tube, 1·25 cm from end. Slide card and wire through, untaped side nearest end. Poke loose wire down barrel.

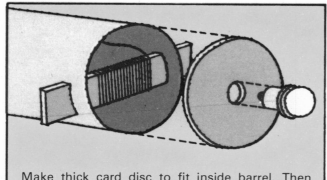

5 Make thick card disc to fit inside barrel. Then make a hole in disc to take bulb.

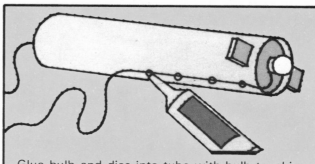

6 Glue bulb and disc into tube with bulb touching fuse wire. Wind another 45 cm of wire round bulb and glue half way down outside of tube.

7 Glue box and small lid on shoe box and make two holes as shown. Thread wire from barrel through holes.

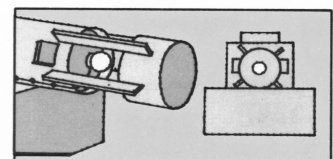

8 Glue barrel to two boxes. Cut 4 5-cm lengths from lolly sticks and glue on 2·5 cm piece of tube. Glue to end of barrel.

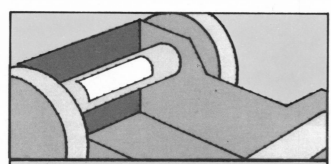

9 Glue a 2·5 x 7·5 cm piece of foil cut from pie dish to one tube. Slide through rear holes and glue a jar lid to each end.

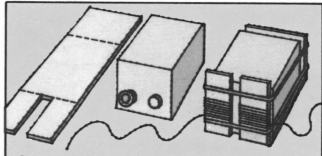

10 Cut and fold card as shown. Wind wire round flaps at one end, leaving approximately 25 cm free. Hold in place with rubber bands.

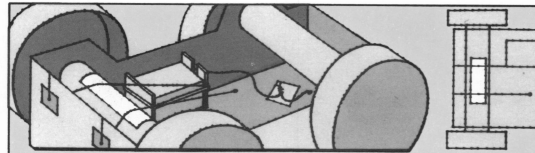

11 Glue battery in box. Twist wire round a wire from barrel. Tape down. Stretch remaining wires over axle and through 2·5 cm slits in back.

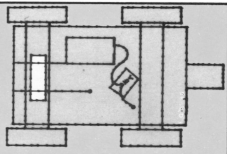

Tape ends to keep taut. Add front axle and wheels. Paint model. Light flashes as car moves along. If wheels slip, put rubber bands round.

Ship in a Bottle

YOU WILL NEED:
a clear glass bottle: approx. 12·5 x 6·25 cm
Balsa wood: approx. 10 x 7·5 x 1·25 cm
stiff white paper: 15 x 7·5 cm
paints · craft knife · steel rule
medium and fine sandpaper
piano wire 40 cm long
flat stick 25 x 0·5 cm long
pliers · strong glue
scissors · pencil · 3 wooden cocktail sticks
nail (same thickness as cocktail sticks)

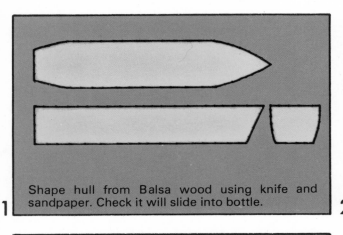

1 Shape hull from Balsa wood using knife and sandpaper. Check it will slide into bottle.

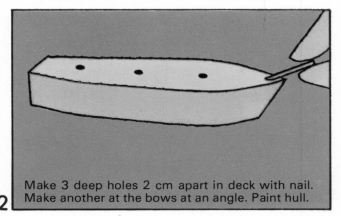

2 Make 3 deep holes 2 cm apart in deck with nail. Make another at the bows at an angle. Paint hull.

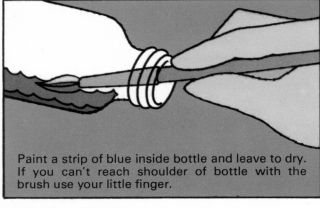

3 Paint a strip of blue inside bottle and leave to dry. If you can't reach shoulder of bottle with the brush use your little finger.

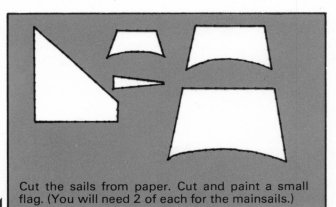

4 Cut the sails from paper. Cut and paint a small flag. (You will need 2 of each for the mainsails.)

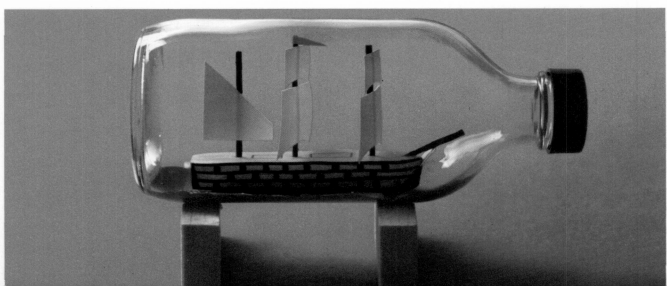

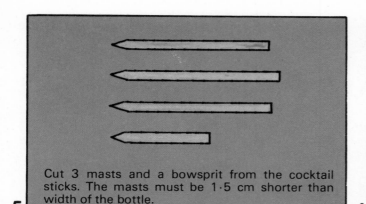

Cut 3 masts and a bowsprit from the cocktail sticks. The masts must be 1·5 cm shorter than width of the bottle.

5

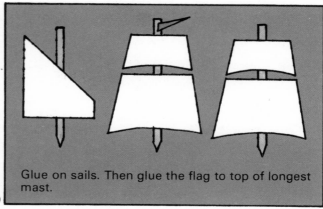

Glue on sails. Then glue the flag to top of longest mast.

6

Glue bowsprit and smallest sail in place. Slot other masts in their holes to check they fit properly. Then take them out again.

7

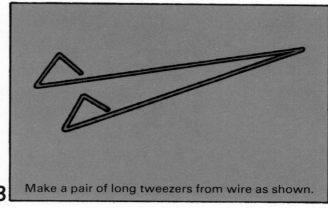

Make a pair of long tweezers from wire as shown.

8

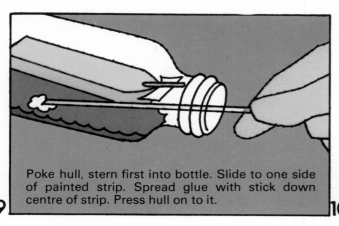

Poke hull, stern first into bottle. Slide to one side of painted strip. Spread glue with stick down centre of strip. Press hull on to it.

9

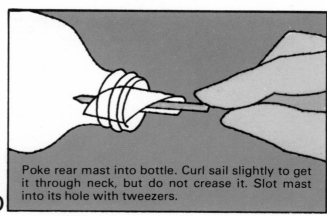

Poke rear mast into bottle. Curl sail slightly to get it through neck, but do not crease it. Slot mast into its hole with tweezers.

10

Put in each mast in turn in the same way. Press top down with stick. Screw on bottle cap.

11

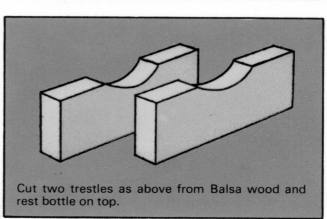

Cut two trestles as above from Balsa wood and rest bottle on top.

12

Cloud Drifter

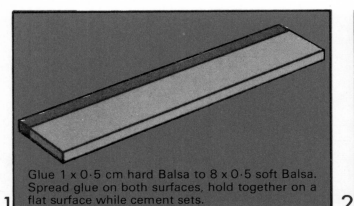

1 Glue 1 x 0·5 cm hard Balsa to 8 x 0·5 soft Balsa. Spread glue on both surfaces, hold together on a flat surface while cement sets.

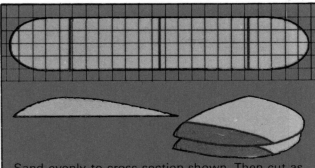

2 Sand evenly to cross section shown. Then cut as indicated. Pin end pieces together. Sand to wing shape (use sandpaper round hardwood block).

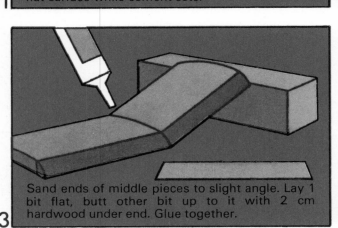

3 Sand ends of middle pieces to slight angle. Lay 1 bit flat, butt other bit up to it with 2 cm hardwood under end. Glue together.

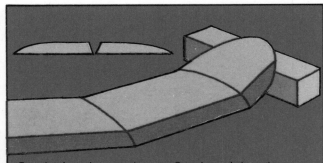

4 Sand wing tips as shown. Sand straight edges at slight angle, glue to centre piece using 3 cm hardwood as prop. Leave each side to dry.

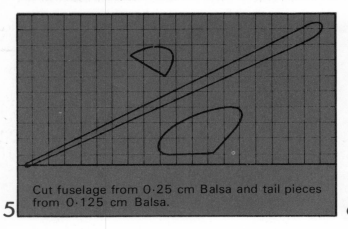

5 Cut fuselage from 0·25 cm Balsa and tail pieces from 0·125 cm Balsa.

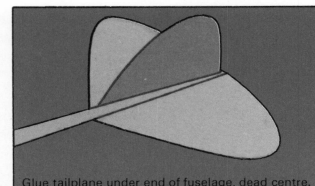

6 Glue tailplane under end of fuselage, dead centre. Glue fin on top to one side of fuselage.

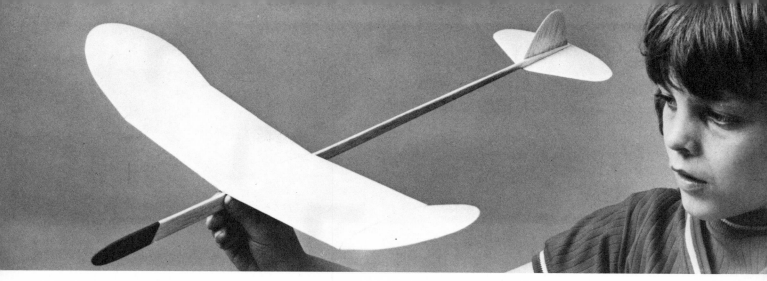

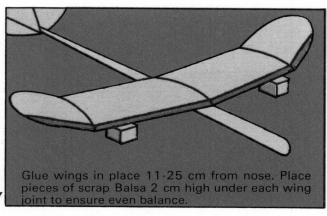

7 Glue wings in place 11·25 cm from nose. Place pieces of scrap Balsa 2 cm high under each wing joint to ensure even balance.

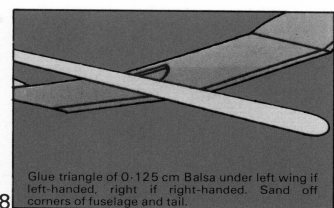

8 Glue triangle of 0·125 cm Balsa under left wing if left-handed, right if right-handed. Sand off corners of fuselage and tail.

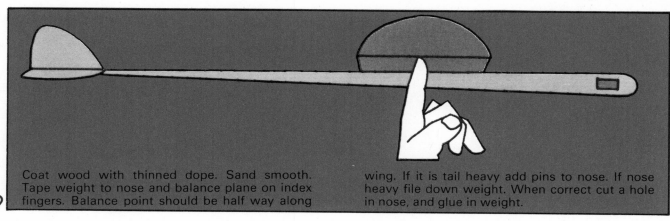

9 Coat wood with thinned dope. Sand smooth. Tape weight to nose and balance plane on index fingers. Balance point should be half way along wing. If it is tail heavy add pins to nose. If nose heavy file down weight. When correct cut a hole in nose, and glue in weight.

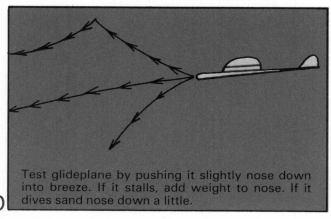

10 Test glideplane by pushing it slightly nose down into breeze. If it stalls, add weight to nose. If it dives sand nose down a little.

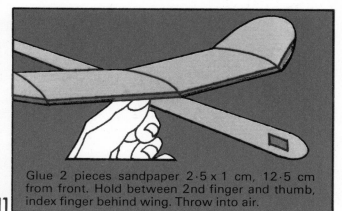

11 Glue 2 pieces sandpaper 2·5 x 1 cm, 12·5 cm from front. Hold between 2nd finger and thumb, index finger behind wing. Throw into air.

Clever Cataplane

YOU WILL NEED:
Balsa wood: 7·5 x 40 x 0·25 cm
glue · craft knife · pencil · sandpaper
steel rule · oil or cellulose paints
empty toothpaste or glue tube
stick approx. 15 x 0·5 cm long · rubber band
tracing paper · pin · scissors

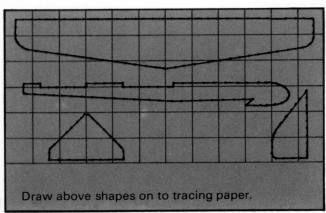

1 Draw above shapes on to tracing paper.

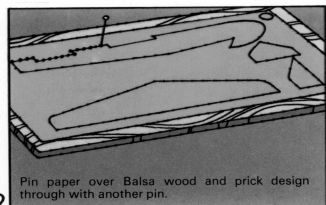

2 Pin paper over Balsa wood and prick design through with another pin.

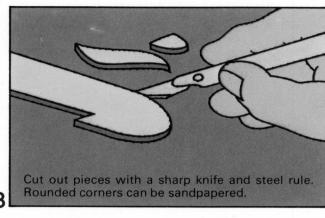

3 Cut out pieces with a sharp knife and steel rule. Rounded corners can be sandpapered.

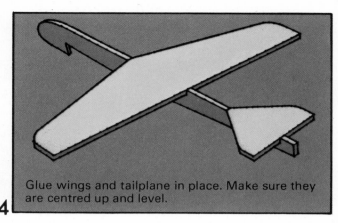

4 Glue wings and tailplane in place. Make sure they are centred up and level.

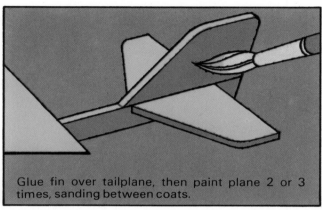

5 Glue fin over tailplane, then paint plane 2 or 3 times, sanding between coats.

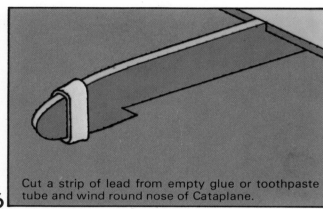

6 Cut a strip of lead from empty glue or toothpaste tube and wind round nose of Cataplane.

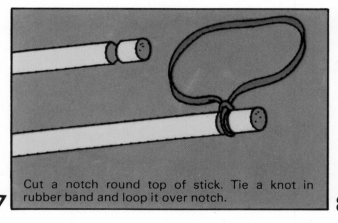

7 Cut a notch round top of stick. Tie a knot in rubber band and loop it over notch.

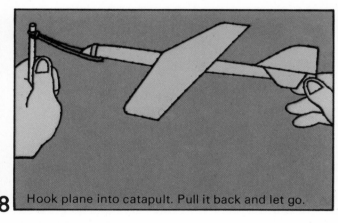

8 Hook plane into catapult. Pull it back and let go.

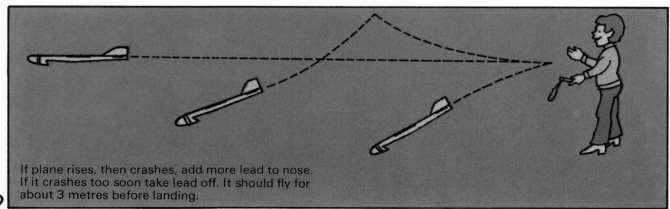

9 If plane rises, then crashes, add more lead to nose. If it crashes too soon take lead off. It should fly for about 3 metres before landing.

Not Just Any Old Junk

YOU WILL NEED:
thick card: approx. 40 x 48 cm
strong flexible card: approx. 20 x 57·5 cm
stiff paper: approx. 45 cm square
dowel or thin cane: approx. 55 cm long
thin dowel 15 cm long · ruler · pencil
hardboard: approx. 5 x 7·5 cm · linen: 5 x 15 cm
ball pen case · 4 flat lollipop sticks
wood: approx. 9 x 1·25 x 1·25 cm · craft knife
strong glue · oil paints · clear varnish
approx. 3lb sand or small gravel
drill and 0·5 cm bit or round file

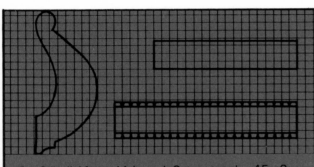

1 Cut 2 'hulls' from thick card. Cut rectangles 45 x 9 cm and 57·5 x 11·25 cm from thin card. Cut wedges 1·25 cm deep every 2·5 cm round large rectangle.

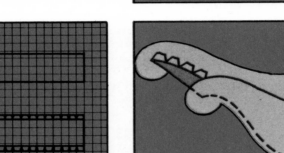

2 Bend flaps up. Glue to hull sides 1·25 cm from bottom. Paint with 6 coats of oil paint or 3 coats emulsion and 3 oil. Decorate sides.

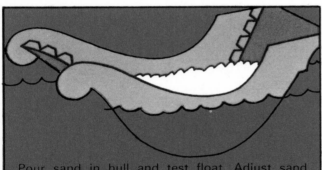

3 Pour sand in hull and test float. Adjust sand content so that lowest point of side is 2·5 cm above water.

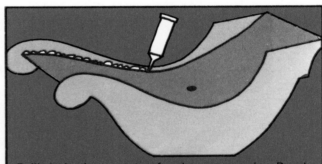

4 Drill hole in centre of other rectangle. Bend slightly, glue to front and back of boat. Squeeze glue into sides. Paint deck with 3 coats.

5 Drill hole through centre of deck and hull bottom 2·5 cm from back. Saw 9·75 cm from pen case. Glue in hole with 2·5 cm showing at top.

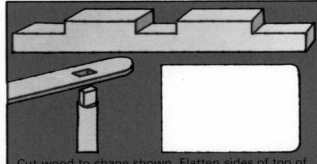

6 Cut wood to shape shown. Flatten sides of top of 15 cm dowel. Make small slot in lollipop stick to fit. Round corners of hardboard.

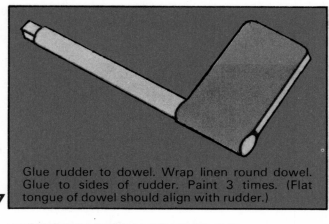

Glue rudder to dowel. Wrap linen round dowel. Glue to sides of rudder. Paint 3 times. (Flat tongue of dowel should align with rudder.)

7

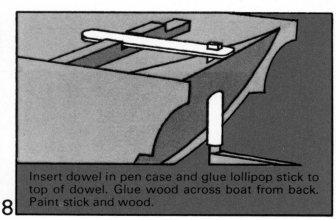

Insert dowel in pen case and glue lollipop stick to top of dowel. Glue wood across boat from back. Paint stick and wood.

8

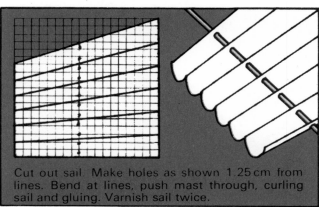

Cut out sail. Make holes as shown 1.25 cm from lines. Bend at lines, push mast through, curling sail and gluing. Varnish sail twice.

9

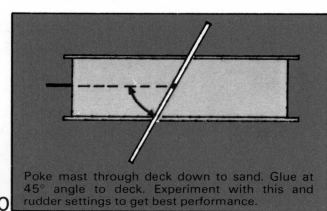

Poke mast through deck down to sand. Glue at 45° angle to deck. Experiment with this and rudder settings to get best performance.

10

Ten~Ton Lorry

YOU WILL NEED:
cardboard box: approx. 9 x 11·5 x 4 cm
cardboard box: approx. 18 x 4·5 x 4 cm
cardboard box: approx. 10 x 12·5 x 4 cm
2 10-cm pencils or dowels
4 plastic bottle caps · Sellotape
4 6·5-cm lids · scissors · craft knife
ruler · fine saw · strong glue
oil paints · scrap card

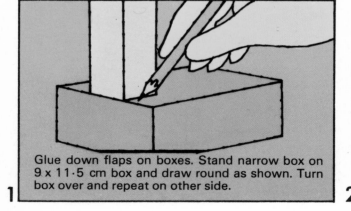

1 Glue down flaps on boxes. Stand narrow box on 9 x 11·5 cm box and draw round as shown. Turn box over and repeat on other side.

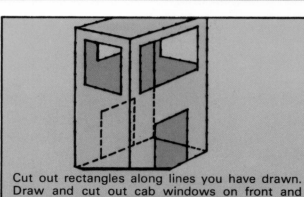

2 Cut out rectangles along lines you have drawn. Draw and cut out cab windows on front and sides, plus a small one at back.

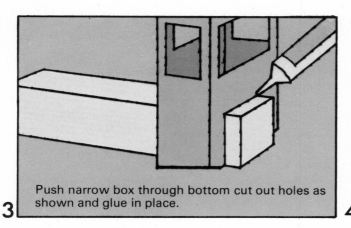

3 Push narrow box through bottom cut out holes as shown and glue in place.

4 Saw off ends of pencils. Make holes in both sides of narrow box as shown and poke pencils through.

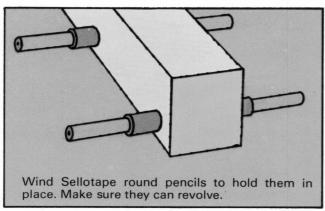

5 Wind Sellotape round pencils to hold them in place. Make sure they can revolve.

6 Cut the largest side from the remaining box and glue box on to your truck.

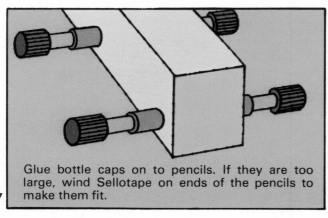

7 Glue bottle caps on to pencils. If they are too large, wind Sellotape on ends of the pencils to make them fit.

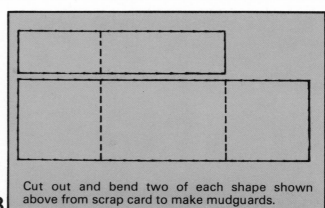

8 Cut out and bend two of each shape shown above from scrap card to make mudguards.

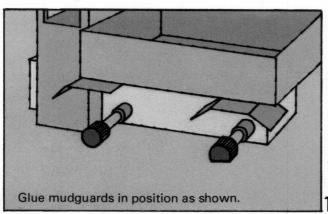

9 Glue mudguards in position as shown.

10 Glue lids on to axles. Make sure bottle caps are in centre of lids. Paint the lorry.

Special Spinna-Copter

YOU WILL NEED:
Balsa wood: approx. 12·5 x 10 x 0·25 cm
Balsa wood: approx. 4 x 4 x 1 cm
dowel or round pencil 15-20 cm x 0·5 cm
fine string: approx. 1 metre long
thick card tube: approx. 3 cm diameter
fine saw · craft knife · strong glue
fine and medium sandpaper · pencil
compass · drill and bit

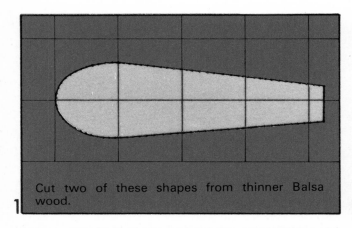

1 Cut two of these shapes from thinner Balsa wood.

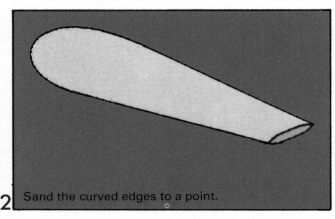

2 Sand the curved edges to a point.

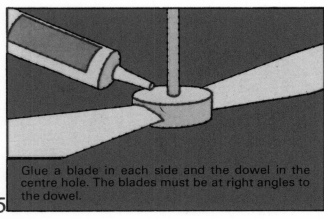

3 Make a disc from the thick Balsa wood approximately 2·5 cm in diameter. Use compass and knife and smooth edges with sandpaper.

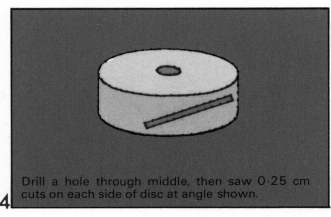

4 Drill a hole through middle, then saw 0·25 cm cuts on each side of disc at angle shown.

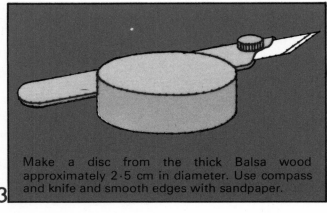

5 Glue a blade in each side and the dowel in the centre hole. The blades must be at right angles to the dowel.

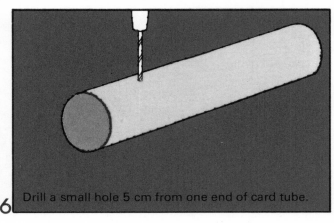

6 Drill a small hole 5 cm from one end of card tube.

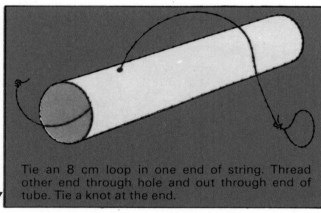

Tie an 8 cm loop in one end of string. Thread other end through hole and out through end of tube. Tie a knot at the end.

7

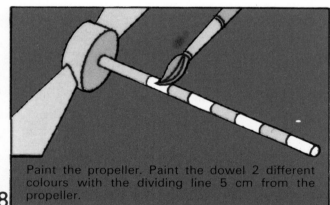

Paint the propeller. Paint the dowel 2 different colours with the dividing line 5 cm from the propeller.

8

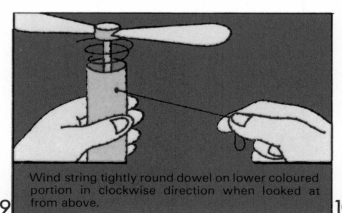

Wind string tightly round dowel on lower coloured portion in clockwise direction when looked at from above.

9

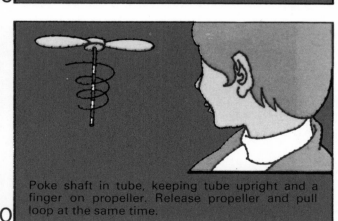

Poke shaft in tube, keeping tube upright and a finger on propeller. Release propeller and pull loop at the same time.

10

Cargo Carrier

YOU WILL NEED:
cardboard box: approx. 20 x 30 x 7·5 cm
hardboard: approx. 70 x 13 cm
fine saw · craft knife · steel rule
2 plastic bottle tops · 4 beads
6 2·5-cm rubber washers · 3 pins · sandpaper
strong glue · paints
stiff card: approx. 30 x 25 cm
2 cardboard tubes approx. 38 x 4·5 cm
round lolly stick or dowelling that
    just fits through washers

1 Glue down loose flaps on box, then cut cardboard box as shown.

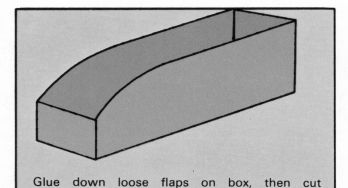

2 Open out remainder and cut a piece large enough to cover the hole with an extra 1·5 cm all round. Then cut and bend as shown.

3 Glue this piece on to box. Start with end flap, then small flaps round curve. All flaps should be inside box.

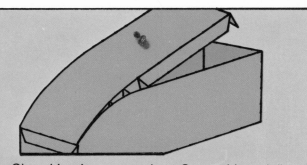

4 Cut wings from hardboard and other pieces shown from card. Round corners where shown with sandpaper.

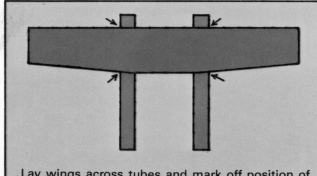

5 Lay wings across tubes and mark off position of wings. Draw another line 4 cm from other end.

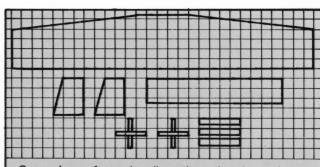
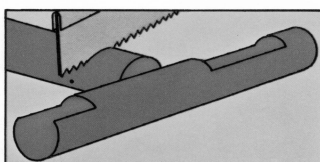

6 Saw quarter of way through tubes at lines. Draw parallel lines connecting ends of saw cuts and cut off pieces as shown.

44

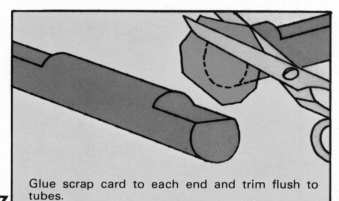

Glue scrap card to each end and trim flush to tubes.

7

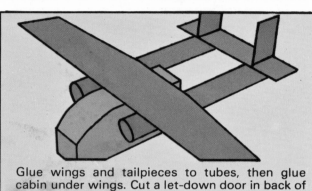

Glue wings and tailpieces to tubes, then glue cabin under wings. Cut a let-down door in back of cabin if you like.

8

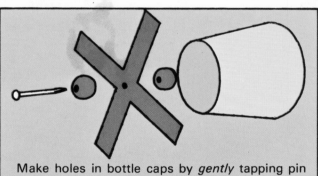

Make holes in bottle caps by *gently* tapping pin through. Then thread a bead, propeller and a bead on to each pin and glue into cap.

9

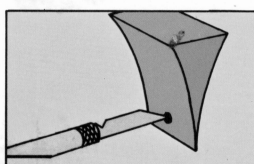

Fold and glue 2 12-cm card strips as shown. Drill a hole large enough to take stick in bottom of each, with knife blade.

10

Cut stick into 2·5 cm pieces. Poke a piece through each hole and glue a washer on each side, close but *not* to card.

11

Glue wheels under cabin, one at front and two at back. Glue on propellers. Paint the plane.

12

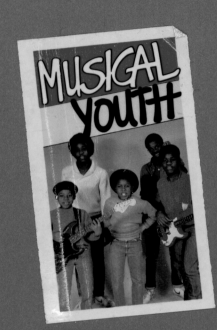

156

151

86

138

First published 1975 by Purnell Books,
    Berkshire House, Queen Street, Maidenhead.
Designed and produced for Purnell Books by
    Intercontinental Book Productions
    Copyright © 1975 Intercontinental Book Productions
Printed in Belgium by H. Proost & Cie

SBN 361 03183 1